LISA SAMUELS

Also by Lisa Samuels

LETTERS, Meow Press 1996
The Seven Voices, O Books, 1998
War Holdings, Pavement Saw Press 2003

Paradise for Everyone

Lisa Samuels

Shearsman Books
Exeter

Published in the United Kingdom in 2005 by
Shearsman Books Ltd
58 Velwell Road
Exeter EX4 4LD

www.shearsman.com

ISBN 0-907562-67-1

The image on the cover is *Untitled*, 1973 (chromogenic development print,
69.22 cm x 67.31 cm) by Gerhard Richter, reproduced by permission of the
San Francisco Museum of Modern Art. Accession number 90.272. Accessions
Committee Fund: gift of Frances and John Bowes, and Mr and Mrs Donald
G. Fisher, Mimi and Peter Haas, and Elaine McKeon. Copyright © Gerhard
Richter.

The author photograph on the rear cover is by Dick Blau.

Acknowledgments

Some of these poems have appeared in the following: *26, Above/ground Press Broadsheet
#186, The Alterran Poetry Assemblage, Antenym, Aufgabe, Court Green, Crayon, The Cream
City Review, Delmar, Denver Quarterly, Five Fingers Review, The Germ, Hotel Amerika,
Jacket, Kenning, New American Writing, New Zoo Poetry Review, Talisman, Traverse,* and
West Coast Line. My heartfelt thanks to all the editors.

Contents

Attest

Fingertips upon the mouth, at last

Complete meaning

Complete meaning

The dragon on my shoulder is hungry again
he watches precisely for the velvet innuendo
that displays him, scent creeping closely
to the torso, room for encouragement –
I see the cloak you draped over the opening
and windows falling forward by degrees,
when emptiness finds constancy and drinks it
deeply down the mouth, forward by the teeth
swishing avariciously like gargoyles –
he eats those too, and sweeps
his baleful eyesight back and toward you,
while you keep walking closer to the moment
he'll chomp you with his customary fires
my sweet acanthine carnivore of hours.

The operator in question

Start with a lapsarian protector, beaten by the brow-born illness.
Insults are the best ones, rigged backward. The jaws of spring are
melancholic, doomed.

This shoe fits both my feet. You managed only to make it unendurable.
Detecting illness requires constitutive vision, listing in reverse, the
order of light underneath us, the mold worn properly across the breast,
like that. I want to take everything off.

In the garden of longing I found you, bent and leaning. You were
grateful and sang a hymn like this:

> "Te de, te di, inlying,
> inscrutable neurons of is.
> You met, you force, belying
> a manner of probably touch."

It was never a tool or an instrument, the hills came and took over. Do
you want to inculcate a steadiness? The scene is far away and the frame
is broken. More acted upon than acting.

Every part of it is alive, scrawls and mangles. Nor questioning what
particular light will turn on the board, the vex, curled and ruminate
for flight. It opens up the skin, belies brown and mutable table tops, on
which we put the plan for this day and try to guess the names for the
next.

I took that garden and folded it up. The earth tore and inebriated itself.
That was a gesture.

Concavity is imperceptible in the dark

intervals of discretion pile up
and she makes pies of them
   for when the strong dilution pours
   and he will not

      leaning over the towers, she made a face
        and making forced

            split giddy in the halters, a hearse of proof

      and his square leaning through the pent-up roof

     lithe monstrance, many-forked positions
      dictate with the sound

        a priori delirium, what waggish innocents

          found underneath their beds, the dirt
           of simpering particularity

    a story: fit within the sides, she squirmed,
      his almighty grooming rented out,
      she declared the ruses inappropriate

    ending porous rounded-off invasions

you mustn't imagine

         something grows

    pre-existence is a leash, it holds the dog under the chin

such frightful pliant tongue-screws set
on the plays of tête à tête

indulgences are those

necessities are these

advancement makes a portrait of the throat, bent backwards
to affix to this important involution a new key, played
clannish on your ordinary back

this ruse is breath, what though it be
a farfetched redolent of

modish parts, extraordinary lush growth
charted from front to

the scene is not a picture, oaken
named, ashen and again

passing by faces

gambit explained as operable

I find that

The rager, the constructor, and the sacrificer

When I go to sleep your conscience talks to me: "wake up!" it cries,
"I have something to tell you!" But when I open my eyes I am always
in that same house, or variations of it: one is set up on a hill,
not known for the grey of its marbled interior, with all the stairwells,
staircases, stairs, vaunting down and upward, circling around,
with always another room beyond. "Do you recognize this one?"
built sideways on the slope of ground around it, flat as a rupture,
only more square, and this one funnels inward to a kitchen or
a function-place, where tightness circles around itself and I am
inside sitting and outside on my way in towards myself.
The waiting. You wouldn't think there was anything in it.
Yours is the creative imagination, constructing the way to see
this further place and the wakeful aspect fumes. Meanwhile,
above ground, I can see the usefulness of playing out each hour for
someone else. Instead of mauling certitude with importunate gestures.
The circumference of the angle is miscalculated because you haven't
taken error into account. Or any roundabout reaching that
you wish for. It is impossible to be clear about something that is not.
There's no reason for you to reckon any of this into the final lading:
when I took your hand it fell like water, and this last gesture is free.
Stable marks are left-hand-sided, the way I turn
toward sleeping in your stead.

The tournament of daybreak

As though secretive, your hair untied
and spun around you like arrested molecules

the tanking earth unyields itself like that
to be in conquest is not, those are seeds of flesh
not escaping nor wanting "the dropping hair

the light-struck eyes full of questioning"
that's a reason to address the issue, waiting for you
here as though forensics were a beginning

I speak to you my love wrestling the page
everything requires muscle like thought is grit
we tell it quick-deep with the slice of eyes

never escaping the designated parts
of your life: one at a time, wheel the elocutions in
and let us look at them once and for all

Nun walking naked out of the ahead of time,
                                     and what she is thinking

The number of fingers needed as fast as possible

the kisses of your mouth sent agonized into the thought-wheel

your hands spun off from the moving car

the spin of the stars sent straight into eyesight

the delirious effect of repetition

canonical manifestations urge through every moment

I have to ask forgiveness for them

forgive me for the despairing impulses I put you to

in order to find from pressure the refinement of nothing

you are pushing me around, and I loathe

every opportunity for evasion

why is it always one or two or three or four, and then

seven and ten and twelve and maybe even sixteen and then

it must be twenty then increments of five take over

like the socks that keep your feet in bondage

rationality is after-the-fact

to make something that doesn't matter against the desire

for matter

requires you to be as empty as the tools

(I never saw her in that posture

but he, many times)

there is no through to get through

the city is as miraculous as the ignorance you say I have

there are collections here in the pockets

you don't see

I was busy making the background as complex as possible

you were drunk with unconscious repetitions

I didn't know the outcome, but I knew the effect

you didn't see the effect

my way is preferable: though the hands are empty

at the end, they are easier to see

you are not you, though you seem so to yourself

pushing me away when the walls come too close

I will push you away when the door is larger

and you fit through it, no through but it

there is no such thing as chaos, there are only variable

descriptions of effects on known conditions

you come screaming up the stairs, knife in hand,

and instantly you are a memory, unreal in the instant,

unsatisfiable

you play some instrument as I walk through the metal door

and I see your eyes like cups of weak molasses

they stick to me

it is memory to escape from and to only the present

which is coming and nothing like

liquid freezing up into hope and honesty and self-compassion

all the attributes that one escapes by dying before dying

there is such an effort to be made to make the body

something in front of itself

I am walking from the cloister with a constant sense

that the wind behind me follows

the unwholesome diction chosen by the forecast

sticking to the skin, the scenes of distasteful passion

myriad bouts of dust and swirling erudition

cloaking the impenetrable stones, the white sucked-out

bones of forgiveness piled up inside the cages

of your serene and prematurely cored self

what I put on even as the cloth shudders

between the revisionary me

and the awful permanent creation of you

there is no way to put it sufficient

to address the cloying majesty that surrounds

and makes a mass of similarity from

the lovely sickened purity of impending desecration,

you put shore-like on the ends of the idea

and me walking fabulously out from the liquid

rise up and make it as keen an exit as wounds

licked bloodily, the body like the church

like the tree, the building fitted airlessly into the bags

of breathing, you can see the air sucked out of her

and vacuum made

her legs grow weak from loss

but so deliciously she keeps on walking, and the trickle

of white grows larger, the possibility of leaving

off maniple and cincture matched

the one who felt

and feeling for her made the possibility of feeling

turn away, what he remembers holds him how the dark

clank and stank made numerous procreations come out

cleaner than the promise might expect

the draining of her fluids

is the slowest seepage kinder eyes can find, looking

everywhere for the other one that walks she walks

with vicious indifference

burning away the skin that lies

around her, no better, no more sighted than he finds himself

upended on the popular style, unable to mark out

whether it makes him better or reviled

though no one knows the insurrection promised him

(she thinks) and here's the dress I wore in previous

transitions, why don't I try it on again and see

what dry dimensions are carved out for me

Upwind

animal pause
the sally paths

unquiet lope
we all should have

a soothing urge
a dining win

the hands taut
round the shape

we're in

Provide, provide

Something for you

Traditionally   harpers
build   fences
like   that   they   know
how   to   "disinvest"   –
or   taking   the   moment
further   than   measurement
we   could   call   it
soporific   sunshine   –
equivalent   your   eyes
getting   dimmer
by   the   year   folding
into   dromedary
lashes   –
under   conditions   we
know   how   to   distinguish
let's   say   the   present
has   no   presence
anyway   what   we   proffer
is   that   voice   rising
to   a   green   invective
still   within   the   leaf
like   piano-eyes
we   took   a   limb   tale
and   drew   it   backward
so   that   you   could   see
the   sketches   saying   "really
I   exist"   and   then
judge,   of   course,
for   yourself

A suitable expression

Invincibly self-destructing, what a swell

    partake of one cue, waiting for

salvific orators to find their honey-hats
  and dump them on our heads.

I thought you made a grand carping
  holiday sound, and it was settled:

we would wind up, toys in the window

    and speak each other's names among the grass.

Even though you thought forsaking
  optimal,

     constant, the rough candy
                  was a little
  more than you desired,

a wanting scene, lapsarian digging

the ground came up all flouncy,

  unserious, your shirt sleeves torn on bread
  left softly next door to the meal,

I ate with conglomerate leanings,
as though a gypsy fit the square with a perfect

    fancy, the laces like

soft cream sides melting next to
paper crisp sterns, all tending to

    what lesson you commenced to make or throw.

It wanted a sirenic and medicinal half-glow,

if only from the tagging underneath:

        I said half-priced, half-meant, imploring
declension had its mark:

it took me apart from thoroughgoing

    certainty, what will in trying
to rescue fire, will lose

    from its split-open side the rhythm, hidden

wrestled so your mark is fixed
upon your brow,

waiting hopelessly for the random clothing

to pronounce silence,
                        silence wanderer,

    she took a vow of absence and remaindered

all her thoughts, she turned them into scoring

rocks and they uphung
                        like glass. It was in fine

    young clusters and made underlings

divine like water, nowhere to find
        the missing throw immodest at the door.

You mocked me with the closet hour before
and still I'm cowed here,
                        any animal
might do a better scene behind

as the smile grows and finds nowhere to go.

Riddle poem

A miss, a mass, a mossy pass, the golden legs undoing, a creature
rare and psychologged, a written fair, a silent fog, for speaking air
the rain does fall, the clouds anew strain out the wrong polarity
brought low to sea, the boat is waiting there.

To see the inner passing by, its slow duress, the silent eye that passes
for an answered spot, a clearance place to fixate more and more.

Of you I cannot name the trance, the footing slips and perishes
the ring is round about the sun, it flourishes taxonomies
and when it's free it will leave off a rhyme for you, a middled bog,
a dull caress plucked daring from the young and scented guard.

Of course a plan is under foot, serene like carpet, meant and struck
beseeching trees to strip their bark and hide.

That is the answer we started with

Glasnost

I made you temporize, but only for a moment.
Glue came unstuck from the roof of your thoughts. Let me
help you with that chain.
Bring it to a pass that will save you from the sheen of
your moral sense. Buff it up and it glistens. I never meant
to make you find a new pattern, only the thoughtrails
descending found us

common rents

altogether, passing

the unbelievable domain shield

I found you in the truck hour
and you were momented

To be more than "for" life and more like "in" it.
To be never slakeful, wrathful, taxing.
I fed it to domesticity and

it was consumed.

I hear your silence, it mounts, like a cliff upon my character.
You fed me candy, whiskey, gullets, and cement, I took them
all in equally.

such passionate pronouncements reveal how
you are learning the language.
I put in foregone words and they elude me

cinematic, providential

moved to fountain

I found you caressing the autobahn, on your knees
and ragged as old film.
If I had been a car I would have put
you inside me.

subject to a ghoulish intensity
she wasted all the unity by screening it

it was a story scene, it stood amazed

cultivate the ruined parts of yourself

forgive me for looking so much like someone
who doesn't understand.

The year collapses (an experiential screenplay)

It was in the dream: a zero centrifugue, concentered backspaced
betrayal, nothing like what I'd seen before, a space in which another
person was wedged but did not stay, the absence of the core was
verified by a high pitched screeching of the upper atmosphere, it
was a private story, it lodged some light into the dark of my closed
eyes, as though I had inhabited a place where someone else had just
been standing and I knew something criminal was going to, was
happening, had happened and was being paid for, only was I paying
or had someone held me there to cover for not paying at all?

It was a residual, contract of betterment or of change.
No one shone the gaslight in your eyes. Darkness reflects it back
strangely better than light which is absorbing and revealing. The
closer you get the more open it appears. And when it's wet it feels
like creasing, the riddle is that this was unavailable.

Sequenced sequins falling at her feet. Instant calumniators crying.
They told the story wrongly and they want another chance.
Wriggling with a circumspect and shadowed look they keep on
peering into the border, asking for remittance. I didn't pay them;
they took it away from me. Never shoed they were, never boarded
mouths.

Youthful indiscretion makes its mark upon your eyes, they become
flecked and jagged as glass scopes flung around the studio when
the fire has been very hot but the artist has no purposes. These
eye splinters make up a totality that shivers on the surfaces around
the walls, they recollect the end of what they might be called, she
made a musical scenario out of the remnants, she found them in the
dream store and had them sold to her by a person who was like a
person who had just been there and was now replaced by someone
who owed her something, only was it a favor or a recompense or a
punishment?

Opine this view, screw it down upon the wood and hold
it with the glue that comes in canisters, no light allowed to touch

it or it fades into mismanageable confluences, like breath held involuntarily, the hand across the mouth so soft and flexible, seeming permanent application of force and the pressure on the throat and the impossibility of speaking, how it seems it will always last forever and does. This particular way of being is as long as it is partial, incremental valediction, pain of shoulders, liquid hands.

It's holding the container to a spout and letting the soft water rush fast down into it by the side of the road that is nothing but a pathway through, it winds and swerves around and other cars declare its reality but it goes – as in, achieves during its ascent and descent, as in, experiences a reason for parting numberless times – nowhere. The light alters on each side and the trees have no reality, they are replaying, as though other trees were just there but have been forcibly replaced, or in the possibility of finding it was another time when the car swerved over the grey surface, with the yellow lines like the flecks in your eyes finding light enough to refract and make the just-replacing asphalt continue.

In the permanence of containment stands the exact moment when the light shifted suddenly away and you found her walking towards you, calling out responsibility, fixing the moment in place with just that light never to be experienced by anyone else standing in that place looking at the water and imagining what it might mean to have the insides transfer and be another inside's inside, the liquid surging and suggesting on its own that it might achieve another form if you could hold your breath and still speak and realize that the moment had achieved its own velocity and could not be contained or possessed with the force of words or motion.

And if you could imagine you were not the person who stood there acting in that way but that you had been entirely emptied out and replaced by another person or the sound of another breath that could have been yours if you had taken it.

Exactly a hundred hours you lay, not knowing the count of time but able to reconstruct it, there with the twig spun out of your lips, trying to conceive that it was a twig and not a projection of your being placed in a circumstance whose measure might be solitude or might be replaceable with the sense that another might be there, too, with you, or you, moving the brows back and forth, descending from the tops of very clear trees down to the burrow that contains what you are not interested in but which you might have been had you been less contained, reaching out to the measure of the other person who stands in that not-quite-circle of a place which is in the open air and yet wrapped in the energy of return.

You might have been the person in the room outdoors, you might have been waiting for someone to pay you or become you, the occurrence is awaited and discharged at the same time. You might have held that energy, it might have been light or space or a corner or an answer, or like the distribution of sentences through time or it might have been like the repeated fixedness of eyes looking through their surfaces to test the reflection that is not more nor less than meaning, the motion of molecules creating a sense full of dream smells or the possibility of being that other waiting, the meeting of stones in air or water, while you look once more as though you could fix appearance in your eyes with a perfectly recallable reality.

I call the motion of those monospheres.

Gathering the screen about her insensible veneer, she was opacity flaked with gold, crumbled and fallen open, rock-like or like a box full of leaves or like a throat losing air or like a man with velvet rolled along his tongue or like a sea vest worn in summer air or like pushing ventricles apart or like a very important article fallen into the air outside the plane or like an idea you have had that like a thought folds back into a light fixture dormant and absorbent so that you have forgotten it and its potency in a completely permanent way.

Charity

The enormous room is full

it is empty

gas houses rise on a horizon
we are in it

through vamping the sound we

locate ourselves downside, the little man harboring
an opportunity inside his waist pocket, screens arriving faster
and faster

people are crowding their ideas, crowing with back wings unescapable
the woman is in charge temporarily, she thrills to it, walls collapsing

through this kind of displacement we

solve something or nothing, it is the same

woman standing to the side with no answers on her tongue
pushing out the skin with bankside cheeks

Connubial bliss

It's curious, how the peaches rise

  with intention

just as novice periwinkle blooms

whether it wants to
or not

in asking for statements of consequence

interruptions formulate the why, because

and smaller grateful runes

a puzzle got by puzzling, nothing inhabited

perhaps pressuring, it couldn't be so

convex, against the weary eyes –

              can you relay
mimesis, or compensate for this

wholly confidential promenade?

The trees lift up their skirts

in answer, assembling

an involuntary set of curves;

but what would it mean to live

in the realm of the voluntary?

Protection's daughter

Historical girl

"Transmatistic" she said, quaffing the words
with a neolooking solar in her eyes, that spoke to him
with I've-been-there beatitudes.

The dubious demon rising on the picture
swayed up to a peak and let us know
the sheets that formed our walls were just for show

and people walking by were looking in
for demonstrated attitudes: she there
with black and white, a color-invested world

sewn in her mouth. It was hard to tell
nighttime from day, the altitudes
were soldered in this place, and there we were

and being there was what we were bequeathed
to do, puppies lingering at our feet,
or stealing kittens from each other in a unique relation

to opacity. It was a story of how one is
with an invisible audience, evadant spires
gleaming in a distance solely in her eyes

as if illusion were "to translate," as distance does
obedience in disappearing ink

A light less dreamed (play for creatures)

A lightbulb crusted in a spider's web at night is no more real
than the light whereby one cannot see it. I said this to the heretic
and he giggled. She spoke then up in the rafters, and her inimitable
crumbling words fell down piece by piece: "I never saw a man as dry
but snow would make him crippled – I never saw a day descry
what nature couldn't see – I never made this place specific,
you neither saw nor adumbrated me!"

> That voice dropped fathoms down the by-light.
> Such glissand where the walls perched, tellingly.

> I listened for the ordinant reply. He said: "I am trying to
discover what it means to be clear. These years are like buckets of water
arranged along the crescent-descending floor. Into each one each day
I drop one drop of the water that is me, and they collect and drain
and dry and I drip in and am replenished. You wouldn't think a simple
stance was so difficult to maintain."

> This was all at variance with knowledge. The heart is stacked
into stacks, and photographic suddenness distempers. It hasn't been
so long since I was moving.

> Lodged like a firefly amidst brambles, the light creates
a forlorn distribution. Not meaning to, not meaning. Constantly
apologizing for unbidden falsity. A figure of oppression stands against
the light, unseeable but for the displacing outline. To communicate
the approach of predictive capacity, he never opened his mouth.
Not to be seen, not to be listened to, but knowledge like a sticking star
brambled in the cloth upon his head. All unawares, unclear.
> Undulating around the cloaked pleasantries, she whistled
down from her cave: "all is immediate. Mediated all. Call for him
and he will answer in indistinct motions, moving even now along."

> This presupposed position, place, lighting, movement,
portions. The denigration of the authentic into dark wires. He held the
unabated air and sensed it back to me, tight and tucked as silver-sheen.
> I keep on waiting for the dream to return, though I know it is
in the sand outside now. They take their places and begin.

Honest and true

Yielding colors adamant
  and forest-like on the drapery

     folding   a long minute
                    aims along the ground

       I found tall stakes
                           manacled

     for your sake

                   absolution in the render
       tenderness in the cure

       out, in the place where
          thing diminishes

                           into space, folds over

——————

     When I hold you on the floor
                           iniquity rushes out

                     sounding the ground
          the difference between
                           what flows to her

     swept gradients in the altering

       She doesn't wish for surety, no
             cloaked futures in the emaciate

but holding one against the other hopes to make

                containment of the friction
generated, half-owned nuance of the given

        what he contested and made a promise of
electing
    the exact nature of the buffer

———————

Lord of rarity, he bends
she diminishes to the sound

slow-smashing up against, ship-like

   in the vested places

       As something to be turned back

   never cratered like that
always predatored

———————

If there were sufficiency elections
  I would vote for you

and then leave, a space

      clattered to opacity

no center offering to contest
what you might find its right to vilify

Agonistic indelibles, archaic absolutes
I write your tournament and you turn
around to pastures bluer and more red

climbing through the pillories
to make my point:

bring your hands over here

I long to make your lips
bear on some particular

spent cellular anatomy

ingested parsimonious delay

The Host of Questions

to live in future
immensity is to declare rhythm catatonic,
that is I see what instruments are flying, inside

out of the collected train, one voice as invidious
as any other stoppage in the fuel lines –

I spoke to you with my body, astounding
ions of willingness no more accurate

than dirt so sure of itself
it mounds the ants into quiescent piles
around it, while they think and think

and think of piling as extension of breath
no lungs, no divisible expenditure offered
the racing front held to the line.

I offer you the flip side of exposure, a leading
fire to flames I already can't see –

you kept the tonnage
surely in containing shapes, your ideas
divining air and offering

portage, serenity, the enclosure
of immense and solid grief – words

kiss flat and grainy, collected bodies
enamored of arrangement, clutched

in collapsing adjutants who have their orders
lingering in the air above their hands –

what did you say?, that I should
dabble partial letters, as serene
and portioned they, as clean as separatism

softly wrangled from the indivisible,
pulling unsuccessfully away?

Progress

The tiger is stuck in ground – he has no instruments

led somewhere, the sky upends

wanting to be like the girl – he is

half-full of sun, a suspended activity not vanquished

the sun is an object, the dream an object – a night

bearing children, underground harvest burbling

underneath – the gourds are shaking slowly in time –

they hold an instrument – I who does –

grown children waiting for nothing they can hold

the ground is weary and not quite flat – you can see

ideas suspended there – I think it warrants

something definite, the footless bird becomes a flower

and open-eyed is hatched there – a woman walks with her gowns

and not, holding the air before her like a stop

In which "resistance" is the operative absence

I was in the well water when you brought
the reasons

"she had a heart, how shall I say?"

dogged, circumstantial

one feature could not recognize the other

though I spoke indefinitely

driven, eyes like stone ruts
mounted on the case

I spent the division, mathematical wind

blew gently over the pieces, the conveyer

flexible as irony

"One can never imagine the product from the blueprint"

Though I waited for you

undevisedly, the snow crept

up under my pillow
smiling

superlative ventilation, through your

iris barred, iris irresistible
syruped with story, prudent

"it *was* all a mistake; I discharged it"

nervous as chandeliers

the bone box of her head could be
unhandled, could extract

color-like cries

Encomium

was the word in the dream: several speechless women
gathered and made a rule of it: where was to be next
and who was waiting?

Everyone was wanting to know what
the word meant, and she was there with her hair

in her hands, holding remnants of the air
they were all speaking.

The involvement of consciousness
with monosyllables, held together
and achieved expanding bubbles inside a nonexistent

space: therefore it is
that your cloak is always larger than the one you imagine,
it covers you and simultaneous articles

in the foregoing, expectation
temporized the body: even air had color and weight,
could be marked by excess volume.

A notion of poison, separation of skin
outwards floating from the inert frame,
this was the house of your embraces, we have breathed out

all the air remains here, repeating itself.
That is the meaning of the word: what you brush back
and find capturing, spreading the distance

of the line, splitting rockface along the teeth
and holding it gently open.

Latitude

the circles rise up toward the air
they are transparent anyway
we look at them through human
hair, barbiturate of rapture

the air is fine of silk
through eyes, apparently
transfigured, refining through
the circular novitiate

the first day once again
assumes a beach, a sand
wealth temperance, I look at you
through human eyes
no different

(Longitude)

(your little feet
disrobe the light
with touches)

(or age itself is differential
lovely, as torpor
interrupts the night

of heat and feet
and lilting eyes
alike)

The Garden of Love

Buildings
beyond the vocational ability of periscopes
derisive green haunts them,

molded avenues
emptiness gone wandering

as though in the dominion of sincerity
a set of eyes.

If he walks with me
but I never hear a word, is that a meaning?

I long to take it wholly in my hand
and find a plan for quietude

the tree I saw is lovely, forming a bowl,
to walk is a version of waking

the messianic foreplay of hours
spent in lacrimose weather.

If recusal is the glowing thing
is that the branch?

Cloak and veil

Iconoclastic relationship to suffering

there is no clean verso to crawl under, anyway nominal

    crisp devolution into status angles, mine and yours
    and the terminal pathos in between

  wrecked integer of head modules, the ones we saw and
  sawing, made wooden
                in other

    words
      gone bad in their fidelity, construed according

         shaped as armlessly as this one

for when the parachute falls, it's no descent at all
not kin, not dementia-held

        but when I found it striking, you were

      not in the air, not plugged in the outlets

entirely unlit schema

     and the wonder was, the wonder was invariable
      upon the limpid projections, none made faster
       then

   immobile in the useless air, the floated body

    and what clings to it

you missed your lack
fell on the back of tensile

many a wraith fell upon her eyes
wholesome diction joining

held and abated

through the interstitial paring off of soul-parts,
welded exponentially together target-like
hear it declared

"mine ore, mine sole, shoe-bar ache
went missing through the hole set up for him
err and sight and glory stench
mattered on the follicles"

when she sings

birds die for lust

a most unfit ontology

where nothing makes, and making bifurcates
pronoun suits, top and bottom

in other

words, she is a he with s's opportunity
no grief spent shuddering

most of all
no finer penetration than such fall

Shock

A closet example: things rise in the air like wings
Against the air, they are

Bent – the air colluding
Abounding, your face arisen through the microscope

In the forehead of cloud
Risen to make you inside, I warrant like a fly

Given to fly, he is what names
The doubled example of story, she is watching

From the sidelines the brain attempts to crawl
Outside the ear, where we have names for it

Audessusdezéro

drinking high levels of stance
liquid, stupefied by greed
for quelquefois, you richness
delecting abattoir, for something
outside bluesome shape, the high
wind slice up there way up in the irretrievable
sky

absolutely incarnate vehicle
distanced like that, soft and co-prehensile
grips the lavish slender partie pris
like that and I and I and that

arriving to the flat wall, désespoir
pouring fluid through the fingers
of one hand to see the real
dimensions of your flesh beneath

oh zéro arrive, show me
that disappearing arc as you turn
credible allons, the languor
streaming underneath your prorated head
some natural evanishment
has pained us late
and I will find you one so we will be

hello and clasping enchantée
the foreign reduction of every
single act I tether
absolutely to your syllables

After the accident

when she walked up to him he said
never aptitude character stalk
what rage what soft, mention me

over there in difference

when and whether

she lie-replied, over
restitution

if only imagine, if only

what makes ripening divided into
"no and please" and no, give me

the chances, rare experiment

collusion of what holds the motion
and choice, equipoise

it makes for the necessity of running, that it should
be running, simple position of the disparate beauties,
sorry and sorrier

necessity of not, ruptured cubical
she flexed her brain

    and he fell out

        belying the daylight,
      what it might give, and giving dispossess

          obedience of disallow

might fall the waking of fall
  be rhomboid, comatose

     shape to sacrifice "the dominion of inside"

   the glee of realization spread over the partition
                   of denial
    shapes of tongue-suck, sporting revolution

          and romanized locutions, the child's

mouth the child's eyes the childspell careening
  off digressions of delay, birch eyes scaled over

      and hands that reach for it

recognizable allowances mean

　　　　　　　　　　　sops to opportunity, the disagreeable runes
　　　　　　　　　stitched into the parlors of her flesh

　　　raged entombments of available light, equipment
　　　　　mentioning bodily gesture, he turned

　　　　　　　　　　　into a thinner version and

　　　　more than insured, found out into the open
　　　　　　　　　　incommensurable avenues of partition
　　　repeated the just

dismay is never more than the particulars of scent
thrown off her torso
　　　　　　　　　　assertions of the paid-for moment

　　　found storage, serving wired-off minuscule embarrassments

　　　　　　up to you, sideways to the hungriest air
　　　　　　　this pique of chosen

into left-off detail, set-aside
emportioning, moved by the angle of judgment

emblazoned portrayal, stuck force
amused within the motion of

and of for then, she wept and small
salt-water dripped across the cliff

then as now, if ever he wanted to make
momentary stalk itself

force genial push out in the meaning
she said to him she said

while I go back

control the moderator, sympathy is the worst part
I walk away I walk and walk and away is
there where you are

fearsome predator of the leaving air
spent waking and spent experience

dangling from the courses

and clearly

meant

The end of distance

I've hardly taken to any life at all
that is a penchant for falling, a syllable
wreathed reckless on the air
that I don't mean, or measuring

has habited us to complicated beds
where we do or do not say the things
we are. I've taken to adjusting from afar

the work we vitalize or will not keep
among us like appropriated tasks
we spill our life across, wanting to watch

what happens when the will is washed
like blue jeans, tightens up, and holds us
clasply in its fit, our haunches rectified
uneven, like something proved by what we have not given.

Target Practice

inarticulate

when you wedged your discriminating

against my frozen link, alnopanity broke through

fhor whene it happened and thene som

touk for fan and youthful opine

fearsome inopera

able to say, not able too preyed operatic

you sliver, you mean, into plithe

never for granting, tunes ravage

inundorable, inappelate, droll and stew

polisinate indemnity, not what you said

forthwrit, and faith is a welded container

into rillsome cracking, upon antediluvian expenditures

crawl, and seethe the imperslippable

furnishings, lithosomatose limbs strewn

up and flipped across the tent of justice

light winds pissspray upon the legible contentments

door opening, flapping through the entrust

and then

you miffed the quiable ventriloquist, he fled

and voice pieces dropping around

the apertured informable leggings, folded out

on the hood of your bronzed and inexplicable

shearing, but then necessity decayed

and you swung over the newly ossified

portrayal, not sung to the two inclines

unhot hats off nip trough wire, to keep the heads

within, poor dear underbelly of worldliness, how it trawls

through the water of adequacy, dragging whiplash tails

behind and cutting through her whining wail

and gaunt meretricious cut-sized and unstoppable

mini-throat, how it spins with egregious air

winning through, unpersuadable, untabled,

and she is mindness itself, phelped and unignitable,

sput and withered, no more caution blocks to put

here, no rewarding philostrata to crawl into,

she ducked the undertaking and it scattered

like winged importunates, annealed

and follied, when did you ever insist on this outcome?

entrapment

she was sure to pay according to the sheets that tied

up entrances, along with better eyes, milled androcentric

rowing counters, the same positive implosion,

heart in the bank, dirt on the boards

well-spent, this is not the brain reel

cure, endurance envisioned enmarbled, her throat

is like the throat of many swallows, it flips up

to the windless tune of grass, what I hold

makes fine and coverable lines appear, one fish

at one end, another at the other, an

iniquitous peal of water in between:

we baulked at the conjoining sedentary

momentishness, I sound like you because I am

in the adjoining room, table spread, legs

crossed, a mix of unsatisfiable comment

on your face, I'll take a piece of this, the best

unforested option laid around us, the only

clear and missionless favour

you could win, querulous hands that keep

augmenting the sounds that drop, thick water-like

from your fled and incontestable lips

and I see their irreversible desire

resurrected, a viscous and unordinary day

run through the map, like tearing

chimed and infiltrant magnitude along the side

and trailing it out behind the police car

Attest

"The real suffering of another"

You made the pediments fall out of sight of us we look

and they are sightless – the day is grey and matches

as in flare and burn – sounds grinding around

a hollow of expedience, my arms ache with a preemptive

benediction, a lattice gaze gone gloomy in foresight

his perched solemnized for an occasion I cannot

warrant – these creaks full of lamentation, some

person's gone again and won't be anywhere – a gaze

far from where you're looking now, can't see

when seeing's mastery gone contemplative how I

wish I too could miscreate the fashion of a shadow

given, one thing added to another like you're missing it

Under the accountability tree

I

for there to be   nothing   to be waited for

for augmenting fractures to delay

I've come to make a chasuble of clay

and lodge it solemnly inside your throat

for there to be delivery of comment, stoked brambles,
charred morosity of campfire oils
soothingly placated over the smooth bend
in the smooth river

II

I reached over to the first treatise I could find:
it was snowy, it minisculed.

Your variables are showing, tuck them up
into the finer promises of your shirt.

  Just when the properties seem aligning, the dust came
blowing through the window. It never made a difference, it
catastrophed the white air out of doors. Window fell, door was never
there, and threshold made her feet go. The children wandered, they
made a fine display of purposelessness. It was all beautiful, it shaped
the airless corridor into a place where voices could seat themselves:
they sat on chairs, on linoleum, on the pilings. One was deep, another
light, another made a whistling sound like curtains.
  Suddenly

you underwent, you oversaw

the evening came on like paper

       Not that anything happened. She poured water over her blue
hair and it curled. This was the night when touch blent everything.
The feel of the finger-nail bent backwards.

       Underneath the almond tree, the light gains weight.
       It is portentous, it is missing something.

III

the spark grows in the ceiling and becomes a star

She leant to the side and it went away. The instant tasted like salt-fire.
You can breathe the cust or you can take it down your stomach.

Even when I am bent forwards everything declares itself to be flat.

The dog of the infinite

Like altruism, as though
an atavistic comparison could be
fetching all the honors,
                              free
whirling symmetry fled its openings
downwind, where the wash found
"to its liking" not to bear,
                              I'm honest
when conditions hamper me, and
thorough when the clapping-to
allows. When the hollow circumscription
made its match along the bench,
a decoy watching there
                              provided suture:
can you see diamond-back, her flesh
torn up like wolves and all I'm seeking
exposed along the casuistry, like wool?
The lines are invisible as ice storms,
conditions zoning one wish
                              from another,
what you pay attention to, transparent
and the useful isometric pushing forth.
I'd take it as a striped domain, this is
what you're wearing now,
                              cleverly
provided for, fair weather focusing
and the tripped conventions lapping you
with a warm, dog-like smile.

The blue sky above

Civility is a monster that has swallowed me up
and munches on the middle with a difference

it wants to make the moon swell with continuance
the girls smiling, roads flat and meaningful –

The skies are roads, meaningful, the portion for
bodies tucked – your sweet face harboring

what we have to do and sorrow feet
like roads – hands that turn from each other –
pieces of the body bowled and nothing functional

I think you are an archer lurching through
the air, convincingly I don't exist

earth-tempered, watered-tempered, something
substantial appeared and I went toward it
guiltily pronouncing my unrepair –

Convince me

You broke the lock and took it out

and all collapsing happens

as a consequence, these narrow bars

keep from resting, roof nails thrown

up in the air and bargain falling

down to bargain, attach yourself

to rueful strokes and amble

where they lie. Disparities lie too

although the quantum atmosphere

denies it, all unveiling minutes

spent out softly, they are waiting

elaborate as mollusc eyes, chosen from

among the temper hours, as though

letting go might weave a California in

and you foregrounded headily, like earth

wanders muddy oaks. You wonder how

the sky falls suddenly

meeting slow bewitchment

what you can see held to contest

the pattern in the lading that you can't

save, though you keep placing it

forward in the portage sack, your eyes

consuming the calm illness

that you left me

Mode of transport

in the moving car, temperance, bound by hazy windows
spread the length, we were wondering, dark meant

   warning signs, he sang the note just when
music interrupted, the resting was a clear
inadequacy, to inhabit the form of

no-one whose outline smiles, balance of two places
   worth attending, flowers were disarranged
everything was not-quite-good as metaphor

allegory of option models, multiple figures
lightly push to center
   ruses for attention, the wide car and dark smiles

   what kind of self-fulfillment ranges color and light
seeming touch to follow curves, illumine moving
bodies, those features trained, discovered

imaginative projection is like dimension
lessening, which part of what
speaks should I listen

   I'll find the scarified change, once fallen
image of half, the profile moving away
see if I don't

The rack of consent

The world in all magnificence surrounded by rope –
it protrudes in animundo, flaccid and succulent   like tongues
your lying articles have reached me and the moment
   here, unbraced, as if for turpitude, innuendo

what she said and what was said by her lies
quivering on the floor quite meshed, unseemly
     or then forest-bound – like trees
taken to the side and opportuned
for speaking in a language   I no longer understand

It was – like that – toast, a word for toast
and what we ate crumbling each other
it wasn't meant to reach the same confusion we caused
     infructuous, cohabiting like pears wrecked on a plate

these confiscated two-by-fours have made themselves
a plan, an Avicenna model, *kitab an-najat*
or her mouth open to arrest   those bearing away
     no more attitude than giant or spleened
gently through, world-like, you did and haunted
standing, because the room folds in
     increasingly, and will

As though such names were falling asleep
and the ocean deep as not-sharks
tearing thoughtless up to find you   thus

can we seekingly attest, or in holding implements can
    divide the same – her lonesome fingers splaying helpless
    outward with the lack of things

their softness, blue walls, purple doors collapsing to be
    the car we rode in, the vehicle, stars falling   silent
    and windows opening, like that I cannot –
finding it to be so feckless, ornamental eyemouths
crocheted open with a permanence you gave them
ceding all the mounds, not knowing how
    to rest, or that there is rest –

your teething mind attends itself
an acreage her way, a venial protuberance
inadequate to the occasion – fixed-up, operational
    calling with a farcical sound

It's like something – seasonal – something you have
failed to see at all, not promised
with a fortless option, hands out permanently
molded, policed at an angle, as if "to be" meant
"to be soldered"

At a distance, she was for that,
her forward-seeming invocation folded into flesh –
    "Hail comatose, hail rich and tender whatness
    felt with a mouth full of sockets
    and a creamy solicitude" – dire there, the steering wheel
what silently contains and gently failure to be

there where you are, arms around
the rest of the world in an attitude
of deferential smiling, *kitab as-shifa*, what brings us to
the beach where sand has found a place
optioning like allegories of what has been – unpromised –

Her beckoning eyes, the sand above the ground
flying ceaseless sideways to the shore
where it will sting you with a long and unforsakeable mnemonic:
    I see you, in an outline that no longer fails
    to exist, like so the world unfends itself, or peeks –
arrive and all material is found to be your hands
haunted by avarice   like the superated throat

Prove the animal by rubbing your hands
over the surface without stopping so as
to make the hills ride back and contain you in
a sliding artificial magnitude that measures trembling to be
    the very purpose it wants   the marrow sack a richter
this, convulsion throttle in a fist, I take it you
    abandoned there, what you will serve

Fingertips upon the mouth, at last

The Doctrine of Equivalents

Standing where the instruments allow
one can see distance rising straight up, as if unity

were the last thing on her mind, crawling
through its vestments like
a proprietor checking out the furnishings.

It hasn't been as dutiful growing
restless close to the fire which is cold
in obedience to molecules

the horizon sets itself a limit
grows in clouds and never comes
to be the state of counting, people

fraught and delicate
display their meanings
at the prompt divestment
model that we've come for.

Intuition's seldom clear and then it leaves
behind the slow slurred speech of doing

what you will when incitement's
flush against you, like a pike
pushing into some real place.

I'm after indispensable alternatives
and cluster captures tending frankly for an end:
distribution starving
desire with no tensile strength

as if adequacy were a loom and you
the spinner sent away to make it.

Come as you are

never sea line felt, always a quotidian attitude
the daily this, the nightly that
stuck in me carelessly, the scissors of confinement

no way to parch my mouth more
than your talking fallen
over the glue-amended thickset
and declining sidewalks, stuck

together we wield munitory places to sit, to walk,
finding and found undulating reaches, the leaf fell
knowingly

I arch here with somatic
imaginings, killdeer and amanuensis larking

I remember, moving through the secondary pause
faltered and youthful, it elides

the hands of love coagulant

> *chorus*
>
> water-spider of despair
> fold me to your vacant lair
> skate around my closing eyes
> monumental as a drop
> folded to the candle stop
> when I see you fork away
>
> and tears flowing from your hair
> drop and stoop and follow
> down your frozen feet
> clinging to the empty ground

                    sounds of hollow
                    glaring through the dreaming air
                    spider spider climbing

he said that and then
we were never more
than the isolating wishes

you investigate the total involution
of sight until your eyes concave
into the stilly water of your completely
dark and completely
live brain

Take over

once every seconds we
have no English for "you"

given sanctimony or else
dovetails holding we

don't have a new story
telling us what to tell

you are the glue that holds
my hands together

while I fake autonomy
to spell the simple ruin

of what's making us
speak commonly your own

language, held up in air
it's visible to the struck eye

you want to shape as
shaping makes transparent

cross-tie "centuries"
wheeling the cars backward

to mold what air around
us to a zoom

An American classic

no trace of
        usurper variance

    potion meeting   and then
     aliment conceived

 No, this is the free light

   it amazes your
                  inconsequence, here is one
     meant to salvage

          embroidered
solipsism wielding and

        opinioned in the dirt

   I waited
     a closed room

             bells, instruments,
   "keep thy life"

      the jurisdiction provenance
beneath you

 worrisome and then not

   I saw his face alive
             he spoke in air
past breathing

    the shot was purely theoretical

her ghostly thread left
lightly on

standing in the dark, waiting

lines featured, musical

he walked them
and despaired, respiration finishes

the spring knot, polished high

"To keep the sun away"
and stony brightness, lack

yellow tendrils flowing out
like wind or water by the head

This was a straightening,

unmarked and dark turning, arrayed
past pardon

a model for turning, a model

imaging the cold feature there, dark question

"insistence, I will"

Just as navigation left your insides

protracted, inappropriate, *as though* feeling

finding its way, wholistic

    a brain at every edge

            tendril scavengers
soft teeth there

I remember the shades
walking against the rotation of earth

    by the gardens, inside closed features

  restlessly dividing

        until the masonry took
until rupture, siren ornaments

  "the sea memory"

     unearthed beside you

that was the peeling
away

    Preparation for crumbling, small mouth sent

  to the round

  and there person

  bequeathed. she had a sheet
    attached to her wrist

          and flew

My theme has a poem

ditty

how blighted can do,
what bits covered over with sycamore
came to edge-mount this forgettable
lapse.

take me to task, rumple my laces
this cancels that
and her young face kept watch.

Serious prose

Her eyes were red, her eyes were orange, her eyes were silvery in
the room lights. I kept an arm between us just in case. If the violin
should happen to play at the wrong moment, she might act. Then
her eyes became reflective of mine, so that I could only see myself in
her eyes. That is the spiritual condition of collapse. I am waiting for
something to happen.

Indispensable protagonist enters, left. Look over there to check. Yes.
You have no sense of what it means to cease to be who you are.

The eyes are speaking, as I watch a little mouth opens in each one:

indefatigable condition
of your monstrous bays
sounding like thises
negligible kisses, inoculated
feather burns on each side
on your wingy things,

whisper loudly so I'll hear
inescapable nearness, trudge
tipple over the frosted
protection, who, spell out
your rising throat, come closer

I got as close as I could then the eyes closed.

An operation was in order. An operant order made a dismal prospect
of the hillside, hillfront, as fast as seeming icicles lit daylight. She left

her shoes behind. The tongue of each one turns to me and licks these words into my hands:

> a fonder swift has left its soft
> impedimenta without gloss
> I felt you on my pooled beside
> recidivist

It was all one to me. Her eyes were blue, her eyes were sad, her eyes were bad. The bone nestled too close. I am the carpet of a ghost, wrapped fully around, it offers a cylinder. The house is empty and no birds nest, so sick and crunchy. Just when you thought she colluded, a surprising thing happened.

Inasmuch as the foreshortened order of the day is to be warned, there is no possibility that it sees its own pattern in the aforementioned icicles. Inasmuch as her feet speak to me when she walks, insofar as her eyes are cameras, just the throwing would have made the bones visible. But it didn't happen that way. The contract stipulated a loss, and a loss came.

6 divisions made themselves known. I translated that.

In a happy ending the eyes made warm pools for the words and melted. There is in the lunar cuticle a chronic dispensation. This is the model of what winks at you. Secure as Nova Scotia. Protracted divinations spill over onto the floor. Sola, solar, res culpa, cylindrical manifests, produce the lists and let's get dressed.

The House we Used to Live in

Tombstone, in various:

here accretions, there renewal

"the flowers push up like prairie dogs"

in the ravine, I saw a closet door: it led to another ravine
there's more:
in the arbor I saw a four-square peering child

dressless

And then:

– *"but wait"* –

The ruts have gotten deeper where the wheels spin in the daylight
here is where she stood to take those words.

The seeing-eye defense.

Lagging through

pitched density

it files in: cover

and retreat

space

and the happenstanced
stands there:

unthreateningly, skin wax dripping

and bidding postures
cull the flicked and ascendable
up here!   there is an exit module
it creeps along out of the line of the wrist

Mulled indemnity, avoidance

I came here and you were not ready to speak

clasped protégé, cure warnings
left and wilted

Leaved

the plank shot back
with intention

"the gossamer is heady, more like pregnant spiders"

Woe, then parched, thirst alley
cramped
                    and made into throwaway

            cubes, torn docket
    settlement

                                I don't need to imagine it

    You have noticed "the *articulation* of the joints is *hampered*"
    said loudly

                        A many-storied building rises up
                        the ladder
                        lift the leg, serenely competent

Not the first remnant, but the last, holds the fluids like sandpaper.
Rub it soothingly, it loosens. The water recurrents.

here it is: pre-departure orientation, forensics,
    "impossible to determine!"

      pleased with herself
      sliced with perfume

All the mannerisms are gathered and ready:
this changes, nothing

they're in there with their
emptiness

        the clicked and unstoppable hold
        regrettably sinks

      "the tops are blowing over"
   and the stems are dry

  If you had listened earlier

        covetous and unpersuadable, you turned away
        to looking

            here, it's here

The fruits of conviction

– we slept, ranges accumulating under our heads
as though insomniac votility had met a likeness, orange
and unseemly – I remember vocation is apparent
like a quantity – perfect moon shapes on the wire, shadows
meritous as salt, and then your movement
like the unkind wave that rolls abandonly – the arc
moves slowly through the city, that one
stone single as anapestics, a diatribe of longing
impressed as in "wanting to expire" – the surly clothes
you put on guaranteed, little legions comb the ground –
dark teeth prickling, hirsute in a false despair
the packet lunges and ordains itself –

the words are over there, away from mouths
that speak them – these belong to the table, those walk
across the floor, seemingly picked up by hands –
cumulatively they are – in the mouth, dusty with use
one saturates to take the dirt down or spit it out
onto the fingertips – seventy times a day
looking for the accuracy of blood, one is always
underneath the real, legible apparencies – the glow of her
bright eyes on the piano – barrier of air
that keeps locale a privacy, diminuendo sudden

you are sitting with your feet like lion heads
overtaking, telling the woman in the dream
"there are no people here" – in the climate
riven with perfume, the fruits are marvels
of descriptive engineering – each one designed
to crater in the mouth with sudden fire –

www.ingramcontent.com/pod-product-compliance
Lightning Source LLC
Chambersburg PA
CBHW022201080426
42734CB00006B/537